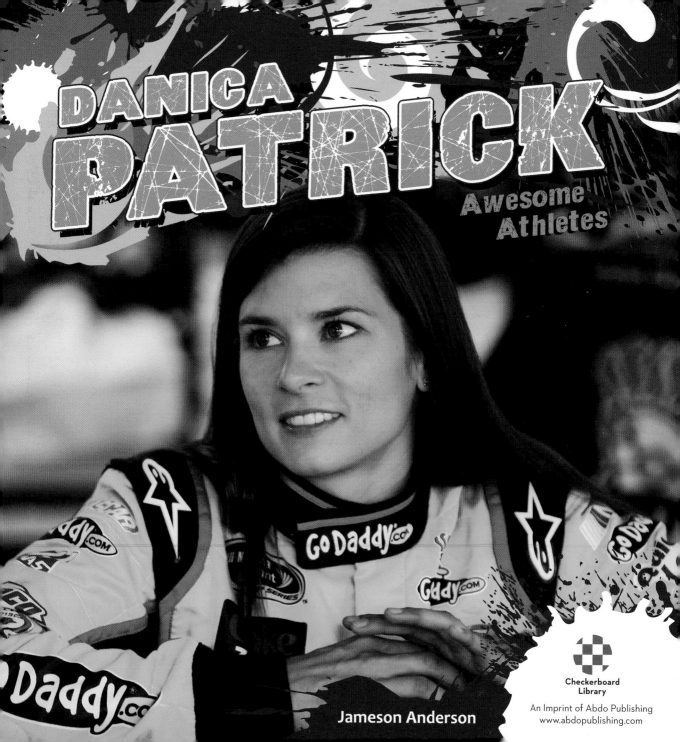

DANICA PATRICK

Awesome Athletes

GoDaddy.com

Daddy.com

Jameson Anderson

Checkerboard Library

An Imprint of Abdo Publishing
www.abdopublishing.com

www.abdopublishing.com

Published by Abdo Publishing, a division of ABDO, PO Box 398166, Minneapolis, Minnesota 55439. Copyright © 2015 by Abdo Consulting Group, Inc. International copyrights reserved in all countries. No part of this book may be reproduced in any form without written permission from the publisher. Checkerboard Library™ is a trademark and logo of Abdo Publishing.

Printed in the United States of America, North Mankato, Minnesota.
052014
092014

THIS BOOK CONTAINS RECYCLED MATERIALS

Cover Photo: Getty Images
Interior Photos: AP Images pp. 1, 11, 17, 23, 29; Getty Images pp. 5, 7, 9, 12, 13, 15, 19, 21, 25, 27

Series Coordinator: Tamara L. Britton
Editors: Megan M. Gunderson, Bridget O'Brien
Art Direction: Neil Klinepier

Library of Congress Control Number: 2014936000
Cataloging-in-Publication Data
Anderson, Jameson.
 Danica Patrick / Jameson Anderson.
   p. cm. -- (Awesome athletes)
Includes bibliographical references and index.
ISBN 978-1-62403-339-1
1. Patrick, Danica, 1982- --Juvenile literature. 2. Automobile racing drivers--United States--Biography--Juvenile literature. 3. Women automobile racing drivers--United States--Biography--Juvenile literature.   1. Title.
796.72092--dc23
[B]

2014936000

TABLE OF CONTENTS

MAKING HISTORY

NASCAR racer Danica Patrick made history on February 24, 2013. Patrick had earned **pole position** in the Daytona 500. Throughout the 200-lap race, she stayed in the top ten racers.

History happened as Patrick entered the ninetieth lap. Nearly halfway through the race, she was in the lead! Patrick held the lead for the entire ninetieth and ninety-first laps. She became the first woman to hold a lead at the Daytona 500.

Patrick couldn't hold on to the lead the whole race. She finished in eighth place. But fans watching from around the world knew that something special had happened. Patrick had proved that a female driver could lead a major race.

Although Patrick (10) placed eighth, it was the highest finish for a woman in the Daytona 500. The previous best belonged to Janet Guthrie, who came in eleventh in 1980.

FUN FACT THE DAYTONA 500 IS OFTEN REFERRED TO AS THE "SUPER BOWL OF RACING." THE 500-MILE (804-KM) EVENT IS ONE OF THE MOST POPULAR AUTO RACES IN THE WORLD.

HIGHLIGHT REEL

Danica Sue Patrick was born on March 25 in Beloit, Wisconsin.

1982

Patrick returned to the United States to race for Bobby Rahal.

2002

Patrick won the Firestone IndyCar 300 in Motegi, Japan.

2008

Patrick became the first woman to lead the pack at a Sprint Cup race during the Daytona 500.

2013

1999

Patrick was offered a sponsorship to race in the British National Series in England.

2005

Patrick became the first woman ever to lead during the Indy 500.

2012

Patrick started racing for NASCAR full time.

DANICA PATRICK

DOB: March 25, 1982
Ht: 5'2"
Wt: 100
Car Number: 10

CAREER STATISTICS:

NASCAR Sprint Cup (SC), NASCAR Nationwide Series (NS), Verizon IndyCar (V)

Races:	56 (SC), 61 (NS), 115 (V)
Poles:	1 (SC), 1 (NS), 3 (V)
Wins:	0 (SC), 0 (NS), 1 (V)
Top Five:	0 (SC), 1 (NS), 1 (V)

AWARDS:

Rookie of the Year: 2005
Nickelodeon Kids' Choice Award for Favorite Female Athlete: 2008, 2012, 2013

A RACING FAMILY

Danica Sue Patrick was born on March 25, 1982, in Beloit, Wisconsin. She is the oldest child of TJ and Bev Patrick. She has one younger sister named Brooke. Danica grew up in the small town of Roscoe, Illinois.

Danica was born into a racing family. Her parents met in the 1970s at a snowmobile race. Danica's father was one of the racers. Her mother was a mechanic who was helping another female racer. TJ and Bev went on their first date together after the race.

Both parents were excited to pass along the racing tradition to their daughters. Danica and Brooke both started racing at the same time. Danica would grow up to be a world-famous race car driver. But it was Brooke's idea to start racing.

Danica and her parents after she finished first in the Firestone IndyCar 300 in Motegi, Japan

FIRST GO-KART

Danica was ten years old when her parents first gave her a go-kart. She had been with Brooke to watch one of Brooke's friends race go-karts. Soon after, Brooke wanted to start racing. Danica couldn't stand her sister doing something she didn't!

Danica and Brooke's father set up a course for them. It was in the parking lot of his glass business in Roscoe. He shaped an obstacle course out of empty paint cans. The sisters learned to drive by steering their go-karts between the paint cans.

On her first try, Danica accidentally crashed her go-kart into a concrete building! Luckily, she was not injured. Go-karts are equipped with safety belts. And, riders wear helmets when racing.

Danica knew that racing go-karts could lead to a professional racing career. Famous race car drivers Tony Stewart and Jeff Gordon had both started as go-kart racers when they were younger.

Soon, Danica and Brooke were ready for a real racetrack. The girls tried out their go-karts at Sugar River Raceway in Brodhead, Wisconsin. Danica immediately fell in love with driving fast and making tight turns on the track.

LEARNING TO RACE

Once Danica was good at driving her go-kart, she signed up to compete at Sugar River Raceway. Danica took part in her first race in 1992. She was still just ten years old.

In the beginning, Danica's father was her **crew chief**. He helped her keep the engine of her go-kart in racing condition. Danica drove a No. 10 go-kart in the races. Later, she would drive a No. 10 car in her NASCAR races.

When Danica started racing at Sugar River Raceway, she was the only girl racing. She is glad that today, more girls are taking an interest in racing.

Just three months after entering her first race at Sugar River, Danica was easily winning races. Sometimes when she finished a race, other drivers still had nearly a full lap to go!

Once Danica could easily win races at Sugar River, her father knew that she needed to race faster drivers on bigger tracks. Danica began to race on tracks around the country.

JUST LIKE DANICA

DANICA HAS VISITED SUGAR RIVER TO MEET WITH GIRLS WHO ARE LEARNING TO RACE. MANY HOPE TO FOLLOW IN HER FOOTSTEPS. THEY SAY THEY WANT TO BE JUST LIKE HER. DANICA TELLS THEM THAT THEY SHOULDN'T TRY TO BE JUST LIKE HER. THEY SHOULD TRY TO BE EVEN BETTER!

GETTING SERIOUS

Danica wanted to race year-round. When she was 13, she asked her father to move the family to California. Her father wasn't able to do that. He needed to run the family's business. But he did help her travel around the country for races.

Danica's family traveled with her to races throughout the Midwest. Danica won races at the **World Karting Association (WKA)** Great Lakes Sprint Series. In 1994, she won her first Grand National Championship. She won the title again in 1996 and 1997.

Danica didn't just win the big races. She won almost every race she entered! In 1996, she won 38 of the 49 races she entered. Danica won first place at the WKA Manufacturers Cup. She won in the junior category against 29 other drivers.

Meanwhile, Danica also had to focus on school. She attended Hononegah High School in Rockton, Illinois. There, Danica was a cheerleader.

Danica also had tried softball and basketball, but racing took up most of her time. In fact, she missed so many cheerleading practices and games, she was eventually kicked off the squad. That just left more time for racing.

WKA road tracks are 1.5 to 3.5 miles (2 to 5 km) long. Road tracks have many curves and are not oval shaped like NASCAR tracks.

CONNECTIONS

In 1997, Danica went to a camp called Women in the Winner's Circle Driver Development Academy in Phoenix, Arizona. There, she met female racers from around the country. Most important, Danica was introduced to Lyn St. James. St. James was a famous female Indy car driver.

At the camp, Danica learned how to prepare herself for a race both physically and mentally. She learned how to be a better driver. She also learned how to talk to reporters and fans before and after races. Danica was getting ready to be a professional driver.

St. James invited Danica to go with her to the 1997 Indianapolis 500 (Indy 500). There, Danica met many famous drivers and other people involved with racing. This included race team owner John Mecom Jr. Mecom saw that Danica was determined. And, he thought she had what it takes to be a great driver.

FUN FACT IN 1992, LYN ST. JAMES BECAME THE FIRST WOMAN TO WIN THE INDIANAPOLIS 500 ROOKIE OF THE YEAR AWARD. SHE CREATED THE DRIVING ACADEMY TO HELP YOUNG GIRLS PURSUE THEIR RACING DREAMS.

When Danica was 16 years old, Mecom offered her a **sponsorship**. He gave her a chance to race in the British National Series in the British Formula Vauxhall Junior League in Europe. Danica was invited to drive open-wheel race cars. These are bigger and faster than the go-karts she had been driving.

Racers Milka Duno, Sarah Fisher, and Lyn St. James, tennis star Billie Jean King, and Danica (*left to right*) at Indianapolis Motor Speedway in 2007

TO EUROPE AND BACK

It wasn't an easy decision to go to Europe. But Patrick's parents knew that she had the talent to make it as a driver. So, Patrick left high school to pursue a racing career in Europe. She lived in Milton Keynes, in southeast England.

Patrick finished ninth in the Vauxhall Summer Series her first year in Europe. In 2000, her second year, she placed second in the Zetek Formula Ford Series. Patrick earned the highest Formula Ford finish by any American in history, male or female.

Yet, Patrick was lonely in Europe. She was making a name for herself, but she missed her family and friends. So in 2002, Patrick returned to the United States to drive for Bobby Rahal.

Rahal and his co-owner, TV host David Letterman, gave Patrick an offer. They asked her to train and race in an open-wheel series. Patrick raced midget cars and open-wheel cars in the Toyota Formula Atlantic and American Le Mans series.

Patrick worked her way up in open-wheel races. She earned a third-place finish in Monterrey, Mexico, in 2003. With this, she became the first female driver in series history to finish on the winner's podium.

Patrick finished third in the driver's overall ranking in 2004. This meant she could qualify for the Indy 500 in the Indy Racing League (IRL). Rahal announced that Patrick would join his Formula One team. She would make her first appearance at the Indy 500 in 2005. This would make her just the fourth woman ever to compete in the race.

In 2002, Patrick raced in the 26th Annual Toyota Pro/Celebrity Race in Long Beach, California. She earned first in the professional category. She beat second-place racer Tommy Kendall by less than a second!

INDY 500

Patrick drove the fastest lap of any driver during practice races for the 2005 Indy 500. During the race, she held the lead three separate times. In her first Indy 500, Patrick completed a total of 19 laps as the race leader. At age 23, she became the first woman ever to lead during the Indy 500.

In the end, Patrick took fourth. She had the fastest finish of any female driver. At the end of the 2005 season, Patrick was named **Rookie** of the Year. She won the IRL most popular driver award in 2005, 2006, and 2007.

In 2006, Patrick switched teams. She joined Andretti Green Racing. As an Andretti team member, Patrick won her first big IRL race.

On April 20, 2008, Patrick raced at the Firestone IndyCar 300 in Motegi, Japan. She decided to skip a **pit stop** toward the end of the race. She wanted to catch

FUN FACT

IN 2009, PATRICK FINISHED THIRD IN THE INDY 500. SHE ENDED THE SEASON RANKED NUMBER FIVE ON THE CIRCUIT. THIS IS THE HIGHEST RANKING FOR A WOMAN IN HISTORY.

At the start of the Firestone IndyCar 300, Patrick was in the third row. She slowly moved up through the ranks, finally taking the lead in the 198th lap. Patrick finished the race in one hour and 51 minutes.

up to the lead driver. Yet skipping the **pit stop** meant she couldn't change tires or add fuel.

It was the right decision. Patrick finished almost six seconds ahead of the next driver. In her fiftieth IRL race, Patrick became the first woman to win an IndyCar race!

In 2008, Patrick also earned a name for herself as a heated competitor. On July 19, Patrick and racer Milka Duno were practicing for the Indy 200 on the Mid-Ohio track in Lexington, Ohio. Duno's car was moving slowly and Patrick wasn't able to pass her. After the practice race, Patrick stormed into Duno's pit area. The argument was caught on video, and Patrick's reputation as a fierce competitor grew.

FAMOUS DRIVER

Patrick has made a name for herself in racing. She is known for her fearless style of racing. And, she has become a **role model** for women in racing. Off the track, Patrick is a well-known advertising spokeswoman.

IRL and NASCAR drivers have **sponsors**. These companies help pay for the cost of building and repairing race cars and traveling to and from races. But Patrick has taken it a step further than most drivers.

Patrick has done Super Bowl ads for her sponsor GoDaddy.com. She has appeared in ads for Secret deodorant, Honda cars, and ESPN. Patrick has also appeared on talk shows and the TV show *CSI: NY*.

All this means Patrick is often treated like a celebrity. Her 2005 marriage to her physical therapist Paul Hospenthal ended in 2012. Many celebrity magazines and talk shows discussed her divorce. Later, when Patrick began dating Ricky Stenhouse Jr., she was again the topic of celebrity gossip. Stenhouse is a NASCAR Sprint Cup Series driver. He drives a No. 17 Ford for Roush Fenway Racing.

In 2013, Patrick won the Nickelodeon Kids' Choice Award for Favorite Female Athlete. She also won the award in 2008 and 2012.

NASCAR DRIVER

In 2010, Patrick made a big change in her racing. She switched from open-wheel Indy cars to stock cars. Patrick started the 2010 season in a partial lower-tier Nationwide Series NASCAR league. She also continued to race in the IndyCar league.

Patrick's Nationwide experience didn't go well the first year. She finished the season ranked forty-third. In the IndyCar series, she did better. But problems with her car led to a tenth place series finish.

In 2011, Patrick finished fourth in the Sam's Town 300 in Las Vegas, Nevada. This was the best finish ever for a woman in any NASCAR race. Yet even with that high finish, Patrick still finished the season in twenty-sixth place.

In August 2011, Patrick announced that she was moving from Formula One racing to NASCAR full time. She would be teammates with famous drivers Dale

FUN FACT IN THE UNITED STATES, NASCAR HAS BECOME THE MOST POPULAR FORM OF AUTO RACING.

Patrick's first Nationwide race was the DRIVE4COPD 300 at Daytona International Speedway. She led for one lap, but ended the race in fourteenth place.

Earnhardt Jr. and Cole Whitt. Beginning in 2012, she would race in NASCAR's Nationwide and Sprint Cup Series.

Patrick's 2012 races had their ups and downs. The Gatorade Duel in Daytona was the first race of the season. Patrick finished trials in the **pole position**. However, she crashed on the last lap of the race.

Patrick again took to the Daytona 500 track in 2012. That year, things did not go well. She was involved in a crash on the second lap and had to end the race.

SPRINT CUP RACING

Patrick moved to the big leagues of racing in 2013. Finally, she was a Sprint Cup Series racer. She drove a No. 10 Chevy SS for the Stewart-Haas racing team.

Racing fans were watching how well Patrick would do. As the first woman full-time Sprint Cup racer, Patrick had a point to prove. She wanted to enter into the series with a bang, and she did.

Patrick again won **pole position** in the Daytona 500. She hit a speed of 196 miles per hour (315 km/h) during qualifying. Patrick became the first woman to lead the pack at a Sprint Cup race. She led for two laps, but finished the race in eighth place.

The Sprint Cup races are broadcast on television around the world. Since Patrick has been racing, her reputation as a competitive driver has grown. She is not afraid to yell at other drivers who get in her way.

FUN FACT AFTER HER 2013 DAYTONA 500 POLE POSITION, PATRICK SAID THAT SHE DIDN'T WANT TO LOOK AT IT AS ANOTHER "FIRST." SHE SAID SHE WAS RAISED TO BE THE "FASTEST RACER, NOT THE FASTEST GIRL."

Some fans say that Patrick doesn't deserve extra attention because she's a female driver. When male drivers lose races, not as many fans talk about it. But as Patrick breaks down barriers, everyone is watching.

Patrick was the first woman to win pole position in a Sprint Cup race. Many of Patrick's races have been record–setting for women.

TAKING THE LEAD

Patrick hoped that the 2014 season would be better for her in the Sprint Cup standings. She knew that there was extra **stress** being a **rookie** in the series. So, she tried to focus on improving her skills for the next season.

Patrick approached her Daytona 500 experience the same as in previous years. She wanted to qualify high and finish the race strong. Again, Patrick led for two laps. Then a major accident got in her way. On the 145th lap, Patrick's car crashed into a wall. It spun out on the infield of the track.

Patrick pushed on through the 2014 season. She had up-and-down races as most drivers do. But unlike most racers, Patrick has all eyes on her. She will always be compared to drivers not just on skill but because of her gender.

In only her second Sprint Cup season, Patrick has proven she can take the lead. Patrick has become an experienced racer who is only getting better. Her fans are waiting for her big Sprint Cup win!

In 2012, Patrick placed twenty-ninth at the ADVOCARE 500 race in Atlanta, Georgia. The following season, she improved by eight places and finished twenty-first.

GLOSSARY

crew chief - a person who is in charge of a race team. The driver gives the crew chief information about how a car is handling.

pit stop - a stop for fuel and repairs during a car race.

pole position - the first car in the starting lineup of a race. It is awarded to the driver with the fastest qualifying position.

role model - a person whose behavior serves as a standard for others to follow.

rookie - a first-year player in a professional sport.

sponsor - a person or a group that provides a sponsorship, or financial support, to an organization.

stress - strain or pressure.

World Karting Association (WKA) - a group formed in 1971 to set the standards for the sport of go-kart racing.

WEBSITES

To learn more about Awesome Athletes, visit **booklinks.abdopublishing.com**. These links are routinely monitored and updated to provide the most current information available.

INDEX